DR. DOORIDDLES
SPELLING

BOOK B1

Associative Reasoning Activities

SERIES TITLES:
DR. DOORIDDLES A1
DR. DOORIDDLES A2
DR. DOORIDDLES A3
DR. DOORIDDLES B1
DR. DOORIDDLES B2
DR. DOORIDDLES C1
DR. DOORIDDLES SPELLING A1
DR. DOORIDDLES SPELLING B1

John H. Doolittle
and
Tracy A. Doolittle

Graphic Design by
Danielle West

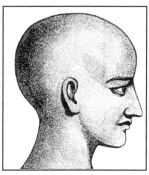

© 2005
THE CRITICAL THINKING CO.
(BRIGHT MINDS™)
www.criticalthinking.com
P.O. Box 1610 • Seaside • CA 93955-1610
ISBN 0-89455-905-2
The individual purchaser of this book is licensed to reproduce
the student pages for use within one home or one classroom.
Printed in the United States of America

ABOUT THE AUTHOR

John Doolittle has been a professor of psychology at California State University, Sacramento since 1966. He received a bachelor's degree in biology and psychology from Stanford University, a master's degree in psychology from San Jose State University, and a doctoral degree in experimental psychology from the University of Colorado, Boulder. At Sacramento, Dr. Doolittle has taught in the schools of Education, Arts and Sciences, and Engineering and Computer Science. He has also been a visiting professor at the University of Melbourne, Australia. Dr. Doolittle is author of a number of books and software published by The Critical Thinking Company, including Riddle Mysteries software, three volumes of Dr. DooRiddles, and Creative Problem Solving Activities A1, B1, and C1.

When Tracy A. Doolittle is not writing riddles, she works for KVIE public television and is pursuing a Masters degree in English at CSU, Sacramento.

TEACHER SUGGESTIONS

Everyone loves the mystery of a riddle and Spelling DooRiddles will bring laughter, groans, and challenges to you and your students.

Thinking Skills

Perceiving relationships between words, ideas, and concepts is called associative reasoning, which is a skill necessary for creative thought. Riddle solving requires students to use important skills of associative, inductive, and divergent thinking to find the answers. Students will learn to recognize important ideas, examine these ideas from different points of view, and then find connections between the ideas. These teachable skills are essential for efficient, successful, open-ended problem solving of all kinds.

Role of the Student

Although Spelling DooRiddles are fun and tantalizing, answering them is not simply play. In order to solve these riddles, students have to generate solutions in many different categories. Students often confuse producing answers in multiple-categories with offering the same answer rephrased. To clarify this confusion, students need to learn how to examine an idea from many reference points.

> For example: If one of the given clues in a riddle were the word horn, students would have to think of different meanings and applications of that word. Does it refer to a kind of musical instrument? A part of an animal? A geographic term? A general horn shape? Or does it refer to an alternative in a dilemma?

Role of the Teacher

At first, the teacher will need to help the students learn how to produce multiple-category solutions by asking higher level thinking questions. Eventually, responsibility of self-questioning should be turned over to the students. Teach your students to ask themselves questions such as: How is the clue used? Why is it phrased this way? How is this clue connected to a clue in another line? How else can this word be spelled? Does this line mean what it says or is it a play on words.

Students should be encouraged to read the riddles carefully, examining individual words, and to use visual imagery to "see" what's happening. As they get into the process of riddle solving, they'll learn to read and weigh the importance of each word in each line in order to interpret the clues correctly. Students will learn to notice how highly descriptive adjectives, verbs, and adverbs indicate specific kinds of movement or action; and how unusual phonetic spellings and multiple word meanings are used to both hide and reveal the clues.

Always ask students why they chose the answer they did. Don't allow students to just give their answer without explaining the reasoning behind it. When answers are backed up and evaluated in group discussions, class members share their knowledge, connect it to other ideas and explore the concept in many directions to find a "best" answer from among possible multiple answers. By working and sharing information in groups, students who aren't familiar with the culture, or whom lack English proficiency, will expand their knowledge, build more extensive vocabulary, and will be able to apply information more diversely.

Classroom Application

These materials make great sponge activities and are excellent activities for independent, cooperative, or open learning situations. The riddles can be used as part of the daily thinking skill curriculum or for the challenge of the week. The riddles spiral up in difficulty within each book and from level to level so that teachers may select the appropriate level of difficulty for students.

Spelling DooRiddles cuts across curriculum areas and deals with real-world objects and situations. Both teachers and students will find the mind-broadening strategies used in these challenging activities richly rewarding at test-taking time.

ANSWERS

Page 1
Pale, Male
Sale, Tale
Lane, Pane

Page 2
Blame, Lame
Mane, Cane
Cape, Tape

Page 3
Pave, Wave
Pose, Lose
Mule, Rule

Page 4
Tune, Dune
Wine, Nine
Line, Mine

Page 5
Hair, Fair
Deal, Real
Team, Beam

Page 6
Seat, Meat
Weed, Seed
Feet, Beet

Page 7
Road, Toad
Moon, Noon
Hook, Cook

Page 8
Sack, Back
Mask, Task
Fold, Gold

Page 9
Bolt, Colt
Lump, Dump
Bumps, Humps

Page 10
Turn, Burn
Calm, Palm
Camp, Ramp

Page 11
Dash, Hash
Chin, Shin
Whip, Chip

Page 12
Fawn, Lawn
Deck, Desk
Diet, Dirt

Page 13
Disk, Dish
Down, Gown
Gang, Fang

Page 14
Full, Fuel
Hero, Herd
Inch, Itch

Page 15
Lift, Left
Ring, Rind
Vein, Veil

Page 16
Rattle, Tattle
Blond, Blood
Found, Round

Page 17
Hound, Pound
Train, Grain
Gutter, Butter

Page 18
Chest, Chess
Swat, Sat
Trip, Rip

Page 19
Word, Sword
Baby, Bay
Gill, Grill

Page 20
Ill, Hill
Hoot, Shoot
Pool, Spool

Page 21
Spoon, Soon
Harp, Sharp
Store, Tore

Page 22
Pine, Spine
Rat, Rate
Rust, Crust

Page 23
Bait, Bat
Blow, Low
Bead, Bed

Page 24
Burn, Bun
Stack, Sack
Scent, Cent

Page 25
Cart, Art
Hat, Chat
Fowl, Owl

Page 26
Frog, Fog
Hint, Hit
Ham, Jam

Page 27
Flour, Four
Map, Nap
Pet, Poet

Page 28
Mat, Hat
Raw, Jaw
Paw, Law

Page 29
Tax, Wax
Day, Pay
Beg, Leg

Page 30
Gem, Hem
Let, Wet
Sew, New

Page 31
Cob, Bob
Hog, Fog
Lot, Not

Page 32
Bow, Row
Bit, Wit
Snail, Sail

Page 33
Mow, Low
Cat, Coat
Stand, Sand

Page 34
Scar, Car
Hip, Ship
Skim, Ski

Page 35
Skip, Sip
Lab, Slab
Low, Slow

Page 36
Snap, Nap
Now, Snow
Oar, Soar

Page 37
Pot, Spot
Top, Stop
Sit, Suit

Page 38
Hop, Shop
Lashes, Leashes
Trail, Tail

Page 39
Thin, Think
West, Wet
Win, Wind

Page 40
Hum, Chum
Sink, Stink
Mare, Bare

Page 41
Pine, Dine
Rear, Near
Flow, Glow

Page 42
Slams, Clams
Peak, Pear
Battle, Cattle

Page 43
Net, Next
Rush, Crush
Jam, Ram

Page 44
Trails, Rails
Sod, Nod
Nice, Niece

Page 45
Sale, Stale
Shoe, Hoe
Stir, Sir

Page 46
Wink, Ink
Rose, Prose
Bid, Bird

Page 47
Fame, Tame
Mole, Pole
Fake, Fare

Page 48
Race, Rare
Luck, Duck
Stool, Tool

Page 49
Mast, Last
Lot, Plot
Ban, Barn

Page 50
Nod, No
Cab, Lab
Gap, Cap

Page 51
Same, Shame
Send, End
Hut, Shut

Page 52
Slid, Lid
Tie, Tire
Fake, Flake

Page 53
Share, Hare
Lobe, Globe
Wading, Fading

Page 54
Rush, Hush
Woven, Oven
Fossil, Foil

MODEL LESSON

Riddles are made up of phrases and sentences that contain clues to the answer.

I'm like a butterfly,
But with a dull display;
And if you add an N,
Think April, June, or May.

For example:

In line one, the clue is I'm like a butterfly. Is it a flying thing like a kite? Or something with wings?

Line two, but with a dull display, gives you another clue. The words dull display implies how a thing looks. What things look like a butterfly but not as brightly colored?

Going to line three, you're told to add an N to your first word. Where in the word will you put that N to make another word?

Line four, think April, June, or May, names months in the year. What is it about April, June or May that makes you think of a single word?

To solve these Spelling DooRiddles, you need to think of more than one possibility. You'll need to look for relationships between the descriptions in the clues and possible words that meet those descriptions. This is called associative thinking. It's also creative thinking because you must generate different possible answers in order to find the right one. Let's look at the clues again.

Clue one in the first line tells you the word is something like a butterfly. This could mean several different things: does it have wings and fly? Is it something that has different bright colors? Is it something that starts as one thing and turns into something else? You need the clues found in the second line to figure this out. But with a dull display tells you that the similarity to a butterfly is in appearance or display, but dull rather than bright. A moth would seem to fit these clues so far, but an army airplane that's painted in camouflage would, too.

The third line, if you add an N, means putting an N somewhere in the first word to make a new word. You could work with moth or plane to make new words, or go on to the fourth line for the final clue. It is think April, June or May, which are months in the year. They don't all fall in spring or summer, so it doesn't refer to time of year. But the word month is very close to moth. As a matter of fact, only an N separates them. Surprise, the two words are **moth** and **month**!

Someone else could come up with a different answer, but since both words need to work together with all the clues, it's unlikely any other answer will work.

Not all Spelling DooRiddles fit the pattern of two lines for one word and two for the second word, but you'll still have enough information to solve the riddle.

His skin is very light,
Without a trace of tan;
Now change the P to M,
And I'm a boy or man.

What am I? ....

A time for shopping sprees,
When lots of things are sold;
Switch S to T and I'm,
A story to be told.

What am I? ....

I'm part of any road,
Change me if you would pass;
Now change the L to P,
And I'm a sheet of glass.

What am I? ....

He did it – not me!
A charge that one might blurt;
Now take away the B,
His walk shows his leg's hurt.

What am I? ....

I am a horse's hair,
I'm long and I am thick;
But change the M to C,
And I'm a walking stick.

What am I? ....

Another word for cloak,
You wrap yourself in me;
I'll mend that paper's tear,
If you've changed C to T.

What am I? ....

© 2005 The Critical Thinking Co. • www.CriticalThinking.com • 800-458-4849

To cover up the street,
Some say asphalt is best;
Make P a W,
An ocean's moving crest.

What am I? ....

I'm what the models do,
Camera shots begin;
Now change the P to L,
I mean you do not win.

What am I? ....

Half of me is donkey,
And half of me is horse;
Switch M to R and I,
Am what kings do, of course.

What am I? ....

© 2005 The Critical Thinking Co. • www.CriticalThinking.com • 800-458-4849

I am a melody,
You whistle when you will;
Replace the T with D,
And I'm a sandy hill.

What am I? ....

Although I'm made from grapes,
A grown-up drink am I;
Change W to N,
Of ten I am one shy.

What am I? ....

To get into the show,
You'll have to stand in me;
With M replacing L,
I'm where some gold could be.

What am I? ....

© 2005 The Critical Thinking Co. • www.CriticalThinking.com • 800-458-4849

I look good on your head,
But not good in your soup;
Just change my H to F,
I'm just to every group.

What am I? ....

A bargain has been reached,
And both sides can be merry;
When D becomes an R,
I'm not imaginary.

What am I? ....

A group of players we aim,
To win the game tonight;
Now change the T to B,
And I'm a ray of light.

What am I? ....

© 2005 The Critical Thinking Co. • www.CriticalThinking.com • 800-458-4849

When teacher says, "Sit down",
I am what you should take;
But make the S an M,
Think burger or think steak.

What am I? ....

I am a useless plant,
I'm pulled when I am found;
Change W to S,
And plant me in the ground.

What am I? ....

Three of me's a yard,
Replace the F with B;
A dark red vegetable,
On salads you will see.

What am I? ....

© 2005 The Critical Thinking Co. • www.CriticalThinking.com • 800-458-4849

Another name for street,
Just switch the R to T;
Another name for frog,
Come hop around with me.

What am I? ....

I orbit 'round the earth,
And light up the night sky;
Now change the M to N,
A time for lunch am I.

What am I? ....

If you would catch a fish,
Then have me on the line;
But switch the H to C,
And fix a meal sublime.

What am I? ....

Another word for bag,
But make the S a B;
My pack will hold your books,
And so, leave your hands free.

What am I? ....

You wear me on your face,
And no one knows it's you;
Now change the M to T,
A bit of work to do.

What am I? ....

To fit the envelope,
You bend the paper twice;
With G replacing F,
Rings made of me are nice.

What am I? ....

© 2005 The Critical Thinking Co. • www.CriticalThinking.com • 800-458-4849

I am a lightning flash,
I need a cloud, of course;
But if you make the B a C,
Then I'm a young male horse.

What am I? ....

I am a piece of clay,
You shape into a boat;
Now change the L to D,
A garbage site remote.

What am I? ....

With 'speed' I do slow cars,
So they don't rush right through;
When B becomes an H,
Camels have one or two.

What am I? ....

A change of direction,
Both right and left look good;
Now change the T to B,
What fires do to wood.

What am I? ....

He's clearly not upset,
As peaceful as can be;
Switch C to P and find,
Coconuts high up me.

What am I? ....

A spot where hikers sleep,
One night and then they're gone;
Now change the C to R,
A freeway's off or on.

What am I? ....

A hundred-yard foot race,
Will show the fastest legs;
Put H instead of D,
My browns go well with eggs.

What am I? ....

Another word for jaw,
Your mouth is above me;
But when you switch the C to S,
Then I'm below your knee.

What am I? ....

I am what you hear "crack",
When lion taming's tried;
Change W to C,
A potato slice when fried.

What am I? ....

I am a little deer,
The youngster of a doe;
Now make the F an L,
I'm what someone must mow.

What am I? ....

The floor of ship or boat,
They walk on me at sea;
Where there's a C, make it an S,
At school you sit at me.

What am I? ....

I'm what someone goes on,
To lose some weight, they hope;
Now change the E to R,
And wash me off with soap.

What am I? ....

© 2005 The Critical Thinking Co. • www.CriticalThinking.com • 800-458-4849

C.D. or D.V.D.,
The last D stands for me;
With H replacing K,
A bowl or plate you'll see.

What am I? ....

The opposite of up,
But switch the D for G;
A woman's wedding dress,
That's beautiful to see.

What am I? ....

A bunch of guys together,
Hope they know right from wrong!
Now change the G to F,
A pointed tooth…and long!

What am I? ....

I'm empty's opposite,
The first L change to E;
I'm coal or wood or gas,
For heat or energy.

What am I? ....

I'm someone good or brave,
And kids look up to me;
Now change the O to D,
A bunch of cows are we.

What am I? ....

I'm shorter than a foot,
I'm one of twelve that match;
When N becomes a T,
I make you want to scratch.

What am I? ....

                        © 2005 The Critical Thinking Co. • www.CriticalThinking.com • 800-458-4849

I mean to raise it up,
It may take all your might;
Now change the I to E,
An opposite of right.

What am I? ....

On fingers I am worn,
I'm not worn much on feet;
Then switch the G to D,
An orange part you don't eat.

What am I? ....

A tube under your skin,
Through me your blood does race;
But when you make the N an L,
I cover up her face.

What am I? ....

A baby's favorite toy,
I make a funny noise;
In place of R put T,
A tale told on the boys.

What am I? ....

I'm hair that's yellow-gold,
Now change the N to O;
A red liquid am I,
And through your veins I go.

What am I? ....

The opposite of lost,
But make the F an R;
I'm what a circle is,
I'm not triangular.

What am I? ....

I am a kind of dog,
Use me to smell their trails;
Then switch the H to P,
What hammers do to nails.

What am I? ....

I'm cars that ride on tracks,
Or trestles way up high;
Now change the T to G,
I'm oats and wheat and rye.

What am I? ....

Rain water runs down me,
At the edge of the street;
Try B instead of G,
On pancakes I'm a treat.

What am I? ....

© 2005 The Critical Thinking Co. • www.CriticalThinking.com • 800-458-4849

The front part of your body,
Between your waist and neck;
Drop the T, add one more S,
A game where you say "Check!"

What am I? ....

A word that rhymes with spot,
Means flies should be aware;
Without the W,
Means you were in a chair.

What am I? ....

To stumble and to fall,
Or journey in a car;
Take off that T in front,
A word that starts with R.

What am I? ....

© 2005 The Critical Thinking Co. • www.CriticalThinking.com • 800-458-4849

I'm less than a sentence,
Of letters I am made;
Now put an S in front,
And I'm a pirate's blade.

What am I? ....

I am a newborn child,
Now drop the second B;
An ocean port am I,
With land enclosing me.

What am I? ....

I help the fish to breathe,
When it is in the sea;
Just add an R to G,
You'll barbeque on me.

What am I? ....

Another word for sick,
Your forehead is quite hot;
Now put an H in front,
A mountain I am not.

What am I? ....

To sound just like an owl,
Can be a lot of fun;
Now put an S in front,
The firing of a gun.

What am I? ....

A place for you to swim,
I'm out of doors or in;
Now put an S in front,
A reel for to spin.

What am I? ....

Use me to eat your soup,
With moon I always rhyme;
Now take away the P,
I mean in a short time.

What am I? ....

I've strings that you can pluck,
For music that is sweet;
Now put an S in front,
This knife will cut that meat.

What am I? ....

A place you go to buy,
Upon a shopping trip;
Without the S in front,
I mean you did just rip.

What am I? ....

A holiday tree,
You chop down with a whack;
If you add an S,
I'm the bones in your back.

What am I? ....

I have a long tail and like cheese,
And living in sewers is fun!
If you take my name then add E,
I'm how you score from ten to one.

What am I? ....

When metal decays you see me,
Showing my burnt orange hue;
Add C on my front and then I'm,
That pie shell the cook baked for you.

What am I? ....

I'm the worm on the hook,
So fish will take a bite;
Without the letter I,
In caves, I cause a fright.

What am I? ....

To purse your lips together,
And cool that bite of pie;
If you take away the B,
I'm the opposite of high.

What am I? ....

Above the lip I often form,
A little ball of sweat;
Without the A I am a place,
Where sleep you like to get.

What am I? ....

To set some fuel aflame,
What fire does to the log;
Now take away the R,
I'm bread for your hot dog.

What am I? ....

I'm a tower of quarters,
Or a bunch of hay piled up high;
Take the T from the middle,
A bag for potatoes am I.

What am I? ....

A perfume a lady wears,
I'm what you smell, not see;
Get rid of the first letter S,
A penny is one of me.

What am I? ....

© 2005 The Critical Thinking Co. • www.CriticalThinking.com • 800-458-4849

At the grocery store,
I'm filled with food and all;
Without the C I am,
A painting on the wall.

What am I? ....

Wear me on your head,
When outside for a walk;
Add a C and I'm,
A bit of friendly talk.

What am I? ....

You'll find I rhyme with towel,
Another name for bird;
Then take away the F,
My "whooo" sound you have heard.

What am I? ....

My "ribbit" is quite loud,
It's my own little ditty;
Take away the R,
I'm mist over the city.

What am I? ....

I rhyme with mint and lint,
I mean to give a clue;
Take out the N before the T,
What baseball bats will do.

What am I? ....

I'm meat that's served for dinner,
Or with eggs that are green;
When you change H to J,
In a sandwich, I'm between!

What am I? ....

© 2005 The Critical Thinking Co. • www.CriticalThinking.com • 800-458-4849

A white and fluffy powder,
Some use to make a cake;
Without the L a number,
If one from five you take.

What am I? ....

Read me to find your way,
I can lead you to a treasure;
Change my M to an N,
I'm daytime sleep for pleasure.

What am I? ....

I am that cat or dog,
With whom you have fun times;
And if you add an O,
Someone who makes up rhymes.

What am I? ....

I often say "welcome",
And lie in front of doors;
Change my M to H,
I go on heads, not floors.

What am I? ....

I'm the opposite of cooked,
Like carrots freshly peeled;
Change the R to J and I'm,
The bone your chin's concealed.

What am I? ....

Another word that means,
The foot of a cat or a bear;
Now turn the P into an L,
For rules we obey to live fair.

What am I? ....

I'm the money folks have to pay,
To the government each year;
Change T to W and,
I'm the stuff found in your ear.

What am I? ....

Twenty-four little hours,
Adds up to one of me;
I'm what you do to buy things,
When you change D to P.

What am I? ....

I mean to ask for something,
By saying please, please, oh do;
And when you change my B to L,
I'll bend at the knee for you.

What am I? ....

A stone that sparkles brightly,
Guessing 'rubies' sure won't hurt;
Then make my G into an H,
I'm at the bottom of her skirt.

What am I? ....

I give you permission,
And met rhymes with me;
Change L to W,
I'm the suit you wear to sea.

What am I? ....

Do me with thread and needle,
I rhyme with low, I'm told;
Make my S become an N,
For the opposite of old.

What am I? ....

Think corn on the blank,
The word sob rhymes with me;
Switch my C to a B,
I mean to float in the sea.

What am I? ....

Another word for pig,
Or one who doesn't share;
Change my H into an F,
I'm heavy mist in the air.

What am I? ....

My parking is a place,
Where cars are left all day;
Make my L an N and I'm,
A way of saying nay.

What am I? ....

I mean to bend at the waist,
A gentlemanly hello;
Try R instead of B and I'm,
How, with oars, you make a boat go.

What am I? ....

I rhyme with hit and I'm,
A tiny crumb of the pie;
Change B to W,
I'm humor so clever and dry.

What am I? ....

I am a garden pest,
And haul my house with me;
But if you drop the N,
I push the boat at sea.

What am I? ....

I mean to cut the grass,
Under a bright, blue sky;
Change M to L and I'm,
The opposite of high.

What am I? ....

When happy I will purr,
Then in front of A put O;
I'm something you should wear,
When walking in the snow.

What am I? ....

I am what you must do,
To get up from a chair;
Without a T I'm found,
On beaches everywhere.

What am I? ....

A mark left by a cut,
That took some time to heal;
And if I lose the S,
I have a steering wheel.

What am I? ....

I'm found below your waist,
Your leg hangs down from me;
And if you add an S,
I sail the salty sea.

What am I? ....

I'm milk that has no fat,
But if the M you drop;
I'm gliding over snow,
Until you fall 'kerplop'.

What am I? ....

© 2005 The Critical Thinking Co. • www.CriticalThinking.com • 800-458-4849

You hop upon one foot,
But if K you omit;
To drink a small amount,
Yes, just a little bit.

What am I? ....

I'm a three-letter word,
A scientist's retreat;
And if you put an S in front,
A large piece of concrete.

What am I? ....

The opposite of high,
Then if you add an S;
The opposite of fast,
Is this one hard to guess?

What am I? ....

A sudden, cracking sound,
With cap you'll find I rhyme;
And if you drop the S,
To sleep for a short time.

What am I? ....

Alone I mean at once,
But put an S in front;
I fall in winter storms,
Sometimes more than folks want.

What am I? ....

I'm found on a rowboat,
And I'm one of a pair;
But if you add an S,
I fly high in the air.

What am I? ....

A cooker for the stew,
Or soup, I may contain;
Now put an S in front,
I'm a small mark or stain.

What am I? ....

I am the highest point,
Of any place you know;
Then put an S before the T,
The opposite of go.

What am I? ....

You go from standing up,
To resting in a chair;
Add U and I become,
Matching clothes to wear.

What am I? ....

I'm a short jump or leap,
I'm what the bunnies do;
And if you add an S,
The mall's the place for you.

What am I? ....

The hair upon your eyelids,
But if you add an E;
The leads they place on dogs;
So they cannot run free.

What am I? ....

A path found in the woods,
I'm smaller than a lane;
And if you drop the R,
The rear end of a plane.

What am I? ....

Another word for slim,
A new, more slender you;
Now put K on the end,
I'm what the brain will do.

What am I? ....

The opposite of East,
Then take away the S;
The opposite of dry,
This one's not hard to guess.

What am I? ....

I mean to finish first,
The champion you are;
But put D on the end,
I'm air blown from afar.

What am I? ....

You sing with your mouth closed,
Now in front place a C;
Another name for friend,
Or pal or old buddy.

What am I? ....

The bathroom place to wash,
A face that is dirty;
Put T right after S,
A skunk is known for me.

What am I? ....

I am a lady horse,
But switch the M to B;
I'm what the cupboard was,
When Hubbard went to see.

What am I? ....

A tree known for its cones,
My odor is a treat;
Now change the P to D,
A fancy word for eat.

What am I? ....

An opposite of front,
Then make the R an N;
I mean it is not far,
To there and back again.

What am I? ....

I am what rivers do,
As they head to the sea;
Change F to G and I'm,
The lamplight you can see.

What am I? ....

He does me to the door,
You say, "I think he's mad";
Try C instead of S,
For chowder good or bad.

What am I? ....

A mountain's pointed top,
The view is great from there;
Now change the K to R,
A fruit that rhymes with chair.

What am I? ....

A fight between two armies,
But make the B a C;
Then I'm a herd of cows,
Out on the old prairie.

What am I? ....

© 2005 The Critical Thinking Co. • www.CriticalThinking.com • 800-458-4849

With Inter I'm a place,
Where surfing is just bliss;
Or add an X and I'm,
The one that follows this.

What am I? ....

Another way to say,
You're always in a hurry;
Add C and I'm all smashed,
You'll get it, don't you worry.

What am I? ....

I'm sort of like a jelly,
In a jar, in stores, for sale;
If you change my J to R,
I am a sheep that's male.

What am I? ....

We're paths you find in woods,
And if we lose a T;
We're steel bars used by trains,
"From sea to shining sea".

What am I? ....

A square of dirt and grass,
You lay to make a lawn;
Bob your head up and down,
N's there when S has gone.

What am I? ....

Think pleasant or think kind,
And if you add an E;
I'm what the uncle calls,
The small girl on his knee.

What am I? ....

© 2005 The Critical Thinking Co. • www.CriticalThinking.com • 800-458-4849

A time to get a bargain,
But when you add a T;
I mean the bread is old,
Expired, don't you see?

What am I? ....

I'm put upon each foot,
So you can run and hop;
And if you drop the S,
Use me those weeds to chop.

What am I? ....

The spoon moves 'round the pot,
The soup will be just right;
And if the T you drop,
The title of a knight.

What am I? ....

An eye that quickly blinks,
To signal it's a joke;
Remove the W,
The stuff of that pen's stroke.

What am I? ....

With petals red and sweet,
This flower's great anytime;
And if you put P in front,
Writing that does not rhyme.

What am I? ....

The offer someone makes,
In auctions hoping to buy;
With R put toward the end,
A creature that can fly.

What am I? ....

© 2005 The Critical Thinking Co. • www.CriticalThinking.com • 800-458-4849

To have me is to be,
Well-known as you can get;
Now change the F to T,
A lion you can pet.

What am I? ....

'Though gopher I am not,
I burrow underground;
But switch the M to P,
A stick that's tall and round.

What am I? ....

I mean not genuine,
Not what it seems to us;
Replace the K with R,
How much to ride the bus?

What am I? ....

I mean a test of speed,
Who has the best machine?
Now change the C to R,
And I'm not often seen.

What am I? ....

Another name for fortune,
Then switch the L to D;
My words—just quacks to you,
Mean many things to me.

What am I? ....

I have no back or arms,
Think a type of chair;
But drop the S in front,
And use me to repair.

What am I? ....

I am a ship's tall pole,
With sails for all to see;
Now change the M to L,
All finish before me.

What am I? ....

With parking I'm the place,
Where cars are often stored;
Add P and my story,
Won't leave you feeling bored.

What am I? ....

To make something illegal,
To say "that's not allowed";
With R, I am a building,
Where animals do crowd.

What am I? ....

To agree without any words,
Moving your head up then down;
Remove the D and I'm,
An answer that makes you frown.

What am I? ....

Another word for taxi,
I'm available to you when hired;
Change the C into an L,
I'm where scientists get inspired.

What am I? ....

A space between teeth,
A break from this to that;
Make the G a C,
And I'm a kind of a hat.

What am I? ....

© 2005 The Critical Thinking Co. • www.CriticalThinking.com • 800-458-4849

I am identical,
Alike in every way;
Then when you add an H,
The guilt you feel today.

What am I? ....

To make a message go,
I am what you must do;
And if the S is dropped,
I mean the story's through.

What am I? ....

I am a kind of shack,
With dirt upon the floor;
Then try an S in front,
The closing of a door.

What am I? ....

When you came down the slide,
I am how you got down;
And if you drop the S,
Then I am that jar's crown.

What am I? ....

Laces made into a knot,
A shoe's bow to reveal;
Then you insert an R,
I'm found on your bike's wheel.

What am I? ....

These diamonds and eye lashes,
Now, are they real? No!
And if you add an L in,
We're made of corn or snow.

What am I? ....

To give him half your treat,
A generous thing to do;
Take off the leading S,
And I'm a rabbit, too.

What am I? ....

The bottom of her ear,
Where earrings can be found;
Now put a G in front,
A world map that's round.

What am I? ....

You're walking in the pool,
They've filled up on the lawn;
Change W to F,
And color's almost gone.

What am I? ....

He moves with reckless speed,
And on his face a frown;
Now change the R to H,
And I mean, "Quiet down."

What am I? ....

I'm what was done to thread,
To make the cloth for shirts;
Without the W,
The place you bake desserts.

What am I? ....

I'm a million-year-old bone,
Held in a rocky trap;
Take out my double S,
And I'm a metal wrap.

What am I? ....